THE
FEBRUARY
BABY

THE
February
BABY

★

Noel Streatfeild

First published in 1959
This edition published in 2023 by Headline Home
an imprint of Headline Publishing Group

1

Cataloguing in Publication Data is available from the British Library

Hardback ISBN 978 1 0354 0841 2
eISBN 978 1 0354 0842 9

Typeset in 14.75/15pt Centaur MT Pro by Jouve (UK), Milton Keynes

Printed and bound in Great Britain by Clays Ltd, Elcograf S.p.A.

MIX
Paper | Supporting
responsible forestry
FSC® C104740
www.fsc.org

Headline's policy is to use papers that are natural, renewable and recyclable
products and made from wood grown in well-managed forests and other
controlled sources. The logging and manufacturing processes are expected
to conform to the environmental regulations of the country of origin.

HEADLINE PUBLISHING GROUP
An Hachette UK Company
Carmelite House
50 Victoria Embankment
London EC4Y 0DZ

www.headline.co.uk
www.hachette.co.uk

CONTENTS

THE baby has arrived. Telephones have buzzed, letters and telegrams have streamed in. The baby's father and relations are exhausted with answering questions. How much does baby weigh? How is the mother? Has baby any hair? Who does baby take after? Then at last the news is passed round for which the friends have been waiting. Visitors are allowed. The question now arises, what present shall I take?

Flowers have been arriving since the baby was born. Though it is delicious to be surrounded with flowers when in a hospital or nursing home, it is possible while there to have too many flowers, which never happens in the home. It is, too, possible to try the patience of even the sweetest natured probationer nurse when you hand her the

fifteenth bunch, saying, 'Would you put these in water, please.'

February is a difficult month for flowers. There are of course daffodils, narcissi, and anemones from the Scilly Isles and Cornwall, and if you can pay for them luxurious great bunches of lilac, sheaves of carnations, and armloads of irises from the Dutch flower markets. But most visitors looking for a

present find that what they can afford makes rather a mere little bunch. So what else?

The inclination on hearing that a baby has been born is to rush off to the nearest toy shop, and buy a delicious cuddly animal. My goodness, what a temptation those animals known to the trade as 'soft toys' are. Lambs covered with curls. A blue and pink elephant type of irresistible softness. Or what about that small white cat with harebell blue eyes? But is the toy, however enchanting, likely to

4

please the mother (for the baby certainly could not care less)? The answer of course is 'No,' it is too early for toys, even a rattle.

Then how about something for the baby to wear? But most of us have been unable to hold on to the little coat or shawl we have knitted, or the frock we have made until the

baby is born. We say to ourselves 'She will want to know how many clothes the baby has,' so though we are aware in our secret hearts that our coat or frock, although we followed

the directions in the book, will fit a nine months' baby better than a new one, we sent our gift in advance, and so are empty-handed when the visiting day arrives.

It is of course lovely if we can take a present to the mother. There is no present better than a really smart bedjacket, or pretty nightgown, or as February is invariably cold how about warm gloves for pram pushing? But such presents are for those lucky few who can spend what they like, and how few mothers have friends in that class?

Years of puzzlement has resulted in this book. Mothers of new babies naturally like to talk and think about babies, especially their own. Here then, between two covers, is information about babies born in February. As well, for those still unable to make up their minds, there are suggestions for February names. Most parents have thought of names to fit either a boy or a girl before the child is born, but there are those who have not made up their minds until they are standing beside the font. My maternal grandfather recorded parents who, on being asked the child's name, went into a huddle, emerging to say, 'Urban District Council.' 'You see,' said the father, 'I've just got on to it and I can't think of anything else.'

So here is a present for the mother of a February baby. Knowing whether the child was born under Aquarius or Pisces, and having reminded yourself with what qualities this accident of birth should endow your

child, it is interesting to turn to the list of the famous born in February. For instance, take the 27th, did Ellen Terry, Longfellow, and Sir Hubert Parry, and do Elizabeth Taylor and John Steinbeck need to cultivate self-reliance, which, being born under Pisces, they should? Perhaps they did and do. Anyway, here then for your consideration, mother of a February baby, are, amongst other offerings, suggestions as to the kind of person your child may grow up to be.

NAMES
for the
FEBRUARY
BABY

FILL-DYKE is the farmer's name for February, because it usually rains so much, so the birth signs for February, Aquarius and Pisces, are both signs associated with water. Here are some suggested names to do with water.

Cordelia means 'daughter of the sea', *Iris* 'rainbow', *Marina* 'of the sea', *Meriel* and *Muriel* both mean 'sea-white', *Rosemary*, which Shakespeare said was for remembrance, comes from a word which means 'sea-dew'. Here are two less usual names, *Amaryllis* meaning 'refreshing stream' and *Meraud* 'the sea'. These

three names, *Guenevere, Jennifer,* and *Vanora* mean 'white wave'.

There are fewer boys' names connected with water, but here are four Welsh ones – *Dylan* 'the sea', *Meredith* 'sea protector', *Merlin* 'sea-hill', and *Morgan* 'sea dweller'. *Mortimer* means 'sea warrior', and *Murdoch* 'sea-man'.

The name February comes from the time of the Romans, whose religious rites at the beginning of the month were for expiation of their sins and for purification. Here is a list of girls' names all of which mean pure. *Agnes, Annot, Katharine, Catherine, Kathleen, Catlin, Ines, Karen, Kate, Katrine, Kay,* and *Nesta.*

Mothers who fancy a name meaning 'pure'

could settle for *Enid,* which means 'spotless purity'.

The 2nd February is the day when the Purification of the Virgin Mary is celebrated. There are of course endless variations of the

name *Mary*, which means 'wished-for child', amongst them are *Maria, Marian, Mariann, Marie, Mariel, Marion, Marylene, Marylyn, Maura, Maureen,* and *Maurine*.

The 3rd February is St Blasius' Day. They are unlikely names to pick but *Blaze* and *Blaise* both mean 'royal'. Many other boys' names have that type of meaning. *Basil* and *Cornelius* mean 'regal'. *Derek, Derrick* and *Terry* mean 'folk-ruler'. *Donald* 'world-ruler', *Donoghue* 'brown chieftain', *Emery* 'work-ruler', *Eric* 'ever-ruler'. *Frederic* and *Frederick* 'peaceful ruler'. *Melchior*, if any parents fancy so strange a name, means 'king of light', *Meyrick* 'work-ruler', *Rex* of course 'king', *Richard* 'stern-ruler', *Roderic* or *Roderick* 'famous-ruler', *Walter* 'ruling the folk', and *Stephen* means 'crown'.

The 5th February is St Agatha's Day. *Agatha* means 'good'.

The 14th February is St Valentine's Day. *Valentine* and *Valerian* both mean 'strong', and so does *Drusilla*. *Bryan* and *Connor* mean 'great strength'. St Valentine's Day on the other hand celebrates love, and is associated with mating birds: '... Valentine, the day when birds of kind, Their paramours with mutual chirpings find.' *Avis* means 'bird', *Columbine* 'dove-like', *Jemima* 'a dove', and *Mavis* a 'song-thrush'. Although it does not appear to have a meaning *Linnet* is a charming name for a girl. For boys *Arnold* means 'eagle-strong', *Bertrand*

'bright raven'. *Colin* and *Colman* 'dove', *Howard* comes from a word for 'osprey', and *Ingram* was 'Ing's raven'.

Since February is the water month surnames and christian names of famous men are worth studying for boys' names. Prince Rupert of the Rhine; *Rupert* means 'bright fame'. Admiral Sir Edward Vernon; *Vernon* means 'flourishing'. Admiral Lord Rodney; *Rodney* means 'road-servant'. John Jervis, Earl St Vincent; *Jervis* means 'spear eagerness', and *Vincent* means 'conquering'. Horatio Nelson; *Horatio* is 'punctual' and *Nelson* means 'son of a champion'.

The apostle which legend ascribes to February is Andrew. *Andrew* means simply 'a man', *Adam*, *Carol*, and *Charles* and *Farquhar* mean 'manly'. *Fergus* is 'a manly choice'.

February makes us think of early spring flowers. Jonquils are coming into bud, *Narcissus* or *Narcissa* mean 'jonquil'. In the sheltered hedges violets are in flower, so how about

Violet or *Viola*? As a fancy name suitable for either a boy or a girl, how about remembering the pussy willow already silvering the hedges? *Willow* is a charming name.

GIFTS
for the
FEBRUARY
BABY

IF a godparent or any well-wisher would
like to give a piece of jewellery to the
February baby, the right stone is the
amethyst. Mothers of baby girls will probably
sigh and wish the February stone was of
more value; but it has good qualities about
it, for besides being a beautiful stone, it is
the emblem of sincerity. But here is what
Leonardus wrote about amethysts in *The Mirror
of Stones* in 1750, in which usefulness would
appear to be their strong quality.

'Their Virtue is to drive away Drunkenness;
for being bound on the Navel, they restrain
the Vapour of the Wine, and so dissolve the
Ebriety; they repress evil Thoughts, and give
a good Understanding'.

The pretty old custom of knowing how to

arrange wild flowers in a vase or bunch so that it brings a message is neglected nowadays. If however your baby should receive a bunch of cinquefoil, violets, and primroses, here is what the present means.

Maternal affection (cinquefoil), will watch over (violets) your childhood (primroses).

If your baby was born between the 1st and the 19th of February read pages 26 and 27, but if between the 20th and the 28th, or if you have a leap year baby the 29th, skip to pages 28 and 29.

UNDER
WHAT STARS WAS
MY BABY
BORN?

AQUARIUS
The Water Bearer
21st January—19th February

PISCES
The Fishes
20th February—20th March

ARIES
The Ram
21st March—20th April

TAURUS
The Bull
21st April—21st May

GEMINI
The Twins
22nd May—21st June

CANCER
The Crab
22nd June—23rd July

LEO
The Lion

24th July–23rd August

VIRGO
The Virgin

24th August–23rd September

LIBRA
The Scales

24th September–23rd October

SCORPIO
The Scorpion

24th October–22nd November

SAGITTARIUS
The Archer

23rd November–21st December

CAPRICORN
The Sea Goat

22nd December–20th January

Aquarius, the Waterbearer
21st January—19th February

PEOPLE born under Aquarius are either very strong or very weak, for their power is spiritual, and it remains for them to discover and harness it. They are nervous and thin skinned, often possessing a high degree of artistic sensibility. They are good looking and gentle of voice. As friends they are true, though seemingly detached. Aquarius people have a special gift for character

26

reading, and their invariable kind-heartedness may put this extraordinary knowledge of human nature to work towards humaritarian ends.

For the Aquarius Baby

Lucky to wear a sapphire, a lynx-eye onyx.
Lucky stones are jet, lapis lazuli, black
  basalt.
Lucky metal is lead.
The Aquarius baby's colour is indigo.
Lucky number is 8.
Luckiest day of the week is Saturday.

Pisces, the Fishes
20th February–20th March

PEOPLE born under Pisces are full of sympathy and apt to give themselves up entirely for others. Sensitive and anxious, they are as vulnerable as they are affectionate and loving. Though not lacking in self-esteem, they need to cultivate self-reliance. Unassuming in manner and not at their best in conversation, they are not easily understood and appreciated. They are restless, yet creatures of habit. Their very duality makes the special virtue of Pisces people their capacity to achieve peace.

For the Pisces Baby

Lucky to wear an amethyst.
Lucky stones are granite, sandstone.
Lucky metal is tin.
The Pisces baby's colour is violet.
Lucky number is 3.
Luckiest day of the week is Thursday.

BABIES BORN
ON
THE SAME DAY
AS
YOUR BABY

I S there any special advantage in being born on a particular day? Is there any truth in what astrologers say — that babies born under Aquarius are like this, and those under Pisces like that? Browse through the names on the next few pages and see what you think.

1st   John Kemble, 1757. Victor Herbert, 1859. Clark Gable, 1901.

2nd   Nell Gwyn, 1650. Hannah More, 1745. Havelock Ellis, 1859. Fritz Kreisler, 1875. James Joyce, 1882.

3rd   Mendelssohn, 1809. Dr Elizabeth Blackwell, 1821. Marquess of Salisbury, 1830. Lord Harris, 1851. Lord Trenchard, 1873.

4th   Jeremy Bentham, 1748. Charles Lindbergh, 1902. Sir Hartley Shawcross, 1902.

5th   André Citroën, 1878. Sir Robert Peel, 1788. Adlai Stevenson, 1900.

6th   Christopher Marlowe, 1564. Madame de Sévigné, 1626. Queen Anne, 1665. Sir Henry Irving, 1838. Russell Thorndike, 1885.

7th   Sir Thomas More, 1478. Charles Dickens, 1812. Alfred Adler, 1870. Sinclair Lewis, 1885. Juliette Greco, 1926.

8th   Robert Burton, 1577. John Ruskin, 1819. Jules Verne, 1828. Arthur Greenwood, 1880. Dame Edith Evans, 1888. Lana Turner, 1921. James Dean, 1931.

9th   Field-Marshal Sir Evelyn Wood, 1838. Mrs Patrick Campbell, 1865. Ronald Colman, 1891. Sir Charles Kingsford-Smith, 1897. David Cecil, 1905. Heather Angel, 1909. Jim C. Laker, 1922.

10th   Charles Lamb, 1775. Adelina Patti, 1843. Andrei Vishinsky, 1883. Howard Spring, 1889. Harold Macmillan, 1894. Bertolt Brecht, 1898. Judith Anderson, 1898. Joyce Grenfell, 1910.

11th   Elizabeth of York, 1466. Thomas Edison, 1847. Sir Maurice Denny, 1886. Joy Packer, 1905 (Lady Packer).

12th   Corelli, 1653. Charles Darwin, 1809. Abraham Lincoln, 1809. George Meredith, 1828. Georges Simenon, 1903.

13th Admiral Lord Rodney, 1718. John Hunter, 1728. Talleyrand, 1754. Lord Randolph Churchill, 1849.

14th Camille, Duke of Tallard, 1652. Aleksandr Dargomijsky, 1813. Val Parnell, 1894. Ida Lupino, 1916.

15th Galileo, 1564. Louis XV of France, 1710. Sir Bannister Fletcher, 1866. Sir Ernest Shackleton, 1874. John Barrymore, 1882. H. M. Bateman, 1887. Brendan later Viscount Bracken, 1901. Claire Bloom, 1931.

16th Réné Laennec, 1781. Sir Francis Galton, 1822. George Macaulay Trevelyan, 1876. Katharine Cornell, 1898. Sir Oliver Franks, 1905.

17th   Francis, Duke of Guise, 1518. Horace Benedict de Saussure, 1740. Malthus, 1766. Maria Francesca Rossetti, 1827.

18th   Queen Mary I (known as Bloody), 1517. James Cassini, 1677. Alexander Volta, 1745. Sir Arthur Bryant, 1899. Mervyn Johns, 1899. Phyllis Calvert, 1917. Mary Ure, 1933.

19th   Copernicus, 1473. Henry Frederick, Prince of Wales, 1594. David Garrick, 1717. Sven Hedin, 1865. Sir Cedric Hardwicke, 1893. Merle Oberon, 1911.

20th   Honoré Daumier, 1808. Mary Garden, 1873. Vincent Massey, 1887.

21st   Cardinal Newman, 1801. George Lansbury, 1859. August von Wassermann, 1866. Sacha Guitry, 1885. Cardinal Bernard W. Griffin, 1899. Madeleine Renaud, 1903. W. H. Auden, 1907. Douglas Bader, 1910.

22nd   Mary, Princess of Hesse, 1723. George Washington, 1732. Sir Robert Baden-Powell, 1857. Olave, Lady Baden-Powell, 1889. Edna St Vincent Millay, 1892. Charles, Duke of Richmond, 1735.

Arthur Schopenhauer, 1788. John Mills, 1908.

23rd   Samuel Pepys, 1633. Handel, 1685. Herbert Jenner-Fust, 1806. William Horlick, 1846. Norman Lindsay, 1879.

24th   Pico della Mirandola, 1463. Charles V of the Holy Roman Empire, 1500. James Quin, 1693. Thomas Townshend, Viscount Sidney, 1733. Wilhelm Karl Grimm, 1786. Grant Allen, 1848. Viscount Templewood, formerly Sir Samuel Hoare, 1888. Sir Douglas Copland, 1894.

25th   Renoir, 1840. Benedetto Croce, 1866. Enrico Caruso, 1873. John Foster Dulles, 1888. Air Chief Marshal Sir Arthur Barratt, 1891.

26th   Anthony Cooper, Earl of Shaftesbury, 1671. Victor Hugo, 1802. Flammarion, 1842. Emile Coué, 1857. Fred Ramo, 1866. Major-General Orde Charles Wingate, 1903. Margaret Leighton, 1922. Everton D. Weekes, 1925.

27th   Henry Wadsworth Longfellow, 1807. Sir Hubert Parry, 1848. Dame Ellen

Terry, 1848. John Steinbeck, 1902. Elizabeth Taylor, 1932.

28th Montaigne, 1533. René de Réaumur, 1683. Arthur Symons, 1865. Viscount Hailsham, 1872. Viscount Simon, 1873. Nijinsky, 1890. Marcel Pagnol, 1896.

29th Marquis de Montcalm, 1712. Rossini, 1792. Michèle Morgan, 1920.

THE
UPBRINGING
OF FEBRUARY
BABIES
OF
THE
PAST

A POSITION WANTED

AS wet nurse, a healthy Young Woman, with a good breast of milk, and can be recommended for honesty and sobriety. Address to M. Laine, Streatham Pump House, Surry.

The Times, 1809.

BABY CLOTHES

1563. Clothes for Lady Katherine Gray's child aged 11 months.

'Two coats for Mr Thomas, whereof the one is russet damask, the other of crimson velvet. Of white cloth to make him petticoats, two yards. Of red cloth to make him like petticoats, two yards. Velvet caps for him, two. A russet taffeta hat for him laid on with silver cord.'

State Papers: Elizabeth, Vol. xxxvii, Fol. 27.

THE WORKING CHILD OVER A HUNDRED YEARS AGO

It shall not be lawful for any Person whatsoever to employ in any Factory or Mill . . . except in Mills for the Manufacture of Silk, any Child who shall not have completed his or her Ninth Year of Age.

Employment of Children, 1833.

A SUPERSTITION

A caul is a little membrane encompassing the head found on some children when born. It is thought to be a good omen to the child itself, and the vulgar opinion is that whoever obtains it by purchase will be fortunate and escape dangers.

Brand, *Antiquities*, 1888.

THE NURSERY MEDICINE CHEST NEARLY A HUNDRED YEARS AGO

THE NURSERY STORE-CLOSET . . . A well-ordered nursery should contain a small cupboard, with two or more shelves high up, out of reach of the children. It should contain: —

Cotton wool.

Black sticking-plaster, and goldbeater's skin.

A pot of primrose or other simple ointment.

A bottle of magnesia, ditto of rhubarb.

A bottle of sweet oil.

Lint prepared for use.

Leech-glass.

A glass for measuring medicine, properly graded.

A roll of cloth, cut into strips for bandages.

A small fine sponge.

Sharp nail-scissors.

A knife for spreading plaster.

A roll of soft old linen.

A tin of mustard.

Bran or linseed meal.

Castor oil.

Gregory's powders.

Grey powders.

Ipecacuanha.

Sulphate of zinc.

Zinc lotion.

Alum lotion.

Hartshorn.

Spirit of ammonia.
Prepared chalk.
Diachylon plaster.
Soap plaster.
Poppy heads.
A bottle of myrrh and camphor.
Eau de Cologne.
Manna.
Phosphate of lime.

> Kingston, *Infant Amusements*, 1867.

AN OLD CUSTOM WHICH STILL SURVIVES
SHROVE TUESDAY

At Westminster School, the following custom is observed to this day ... at 11 o'clock a.m. a verger of the Abbey, in his gown, bearing a silver bâton, emerges from the college kitchen, followed by the cook of the school, in his white apron, jacket, and cap, and carrying a pancake. On arriving at the school-room door, he announces himself, 'The cook;' and having entered the school-room, he advances to the bar which separates the upper school from the lower

one, twirls the pancake in the pan, and then
tosses it over the bar into the upper school,
among a crowd of boys, who scramble for
the pancake; and he who gets it unbroken,
and carries it to the deanery, demands the
honorarium of a guinea (sometimes two
guineas), from the Abbey funds, though the
custom is not mentioned in the Abbey
statutes: the cook also receives two guineas
for his performance.

Chambers's *Book of Days*, 1883.

A CUSTOM WHICH HAS DIED OUT

Till within the last twenty or thirty years, it had been a custom, time out of mind, for the scholars of the free-school of Bromfield, about the beginning of Lent, or, in the more expressive phraseology of the country, at Fastings Even, to *bar out the master*; that is to say, to depose and exclude him from his school, and keep him out for three days. During the period of this expulsion, the doors of the citadel, the school, were strongly barricaded within; and the boys, who defended it like a besieged city, were armed with *bore-tree*, or elder pop-guns. The master, meanwhile, made various efforts, both by force and stratagem, to regain his lost authority. If he succeeded, heavy tasks were imposed, and the business of the school was resumed and submitted to; but it more commonly happened that he was repulsed and defeated. After three days' siege terms of capitulation were proposed by the master, and accepted by the boys. These terms were summed up in an old formula of Latin Leonine verses, stipulating what hours and times should, for the year ensuing, be allotted to study, and what to relaxation and play.

Hutchinson, *History of Cumberland*, 1794.

A
ROYAL FEBRUARY
BABY

INSTRUCTION to the royal governess given by Queen Katharine in 1525, concerning the upbringing of her daughter Mary, then nine years old.

'First, above all other things, the countess of Salisbury, being lady-governess, shall, according to the singular confidence that the king's highness hath in her, give most tender regard to all that concerns the person of said princess, her honourable education and training in virtuous demeanour; that is to say, to serve God, from whom all grace and goodness proceedeth. Likewise, at seasons convenient, to use moderate exercise, taking open air in gardens, sweet and wholesome places, and walks, (which may conduce unto her health, solace, and comfort), as by the said lady governess shall be thought most convenient. And likewise to pass her time most seasons at her virginals, or other musical instruments, so that the same be not *too much*, and without *fatigacion* or weariness, to attend to her learning of Latin-tongue and French. At other seasons to dance, and among the rest to have good respect to her diet, which is meet to be pure, well prepared, dressed, and served with comfortable, joyous, and merry communication, in all honourable and virtuous manner. Likewise, the cleanliness and well-wearing of her garments and apparel, both of her chamber and person, so that everything about her be pure, sweet, clean, and wholesome, as to so great a princess doth appertain: all corruptions, evil airs, and things noisome and unpleasant to be eschewed.'

Strickland, *Lives of the Queens of England*, 1842.

DISTINGUISHED
FEBRUARY
BABIES

CHARLES DICKENS
born February 1812.

HE tells of beginning his 'business life' at the age of twelve. The blacking warehouse was the last house on the left-hand side of the way, at old Hungerford-stairs. It was a crazy, tumble-down old house, abutting of course on the river, and literally overrun with rats. Its wainscoted rooms, and its rotten floors and staircase, and the old grey rats swarming down in the cellars, and the sound of their squeaking and scuffling coming up the stairs at all times, and the dirt and decay of the place, rise up visibly before me, as if I were there again. The counting-house was on the first floor, looking over the coal-barges and the river. There was a recess in it, in which I was to sit and work. My work was to cover the pots of paste-blacking . . .

The deep remembrance of the sense I had of being utterly neglected and hopeless; of the shame I felt in my position; of the misery it was to my young heart to believe that, day by day, what I had learned, and thought, and delighted in, and raised my fancy and my emulation up by, was passing away from me, never to be brought back any more; cannot be written. My whole nature was so penetrated with the grief and humiliation of such considerations, that even now, famous and caressed and happy, I often forget in my dreams that I have a dear wife and children; even that I am a man; and wander desolately back to that time of my life.

Forster, *The Life of Charles Dickens*, 1872.

born February 1755.

I was taught to write, when a girl in America, by a soldier in my father's regiment who began life in the character of a gentleman, but, being an incorrigible sot, retained nothing but a fine hand to distinguish him from his fellows when he was chosen my teacher; ... this tutor of mine visited the black hole so often, that I got copies, ... perhaps twenty ... at long intervals, when he was removed into another regiment. I was thus deprived of all instruction of this and of

almost every other kind; but then it was intended to send me to a convent in Canada, where officers' daughters got some sort of superficial education. This was deferred from year to year, and then dropped because we thought of coming home, where I was to learn every thing; but, by that time, I was grown very tall, very awkward, and so sensitive that a look disconcerted me, and I went to no school except that where dancing was taught, which I very soon left from the same miserable conscious awkwardness.

Memoir and Correspondence of Mrs Grant of Laggan edited by her son, J. P. Grant, 1844.

VICTOR HUGO
born February 1802.

He remembers a play put on at a school party. A stage was separated off in the school-room by a curtain. The play was 'Geneviève de Brabant.' Rose was Geneviève, and he, as the smallest in the school, had the part of her son.

He was dressed in tights and a fleece from which hung a claw of iron. He didn't understand the drama and it seemed long. Bored, he entertained himself by using his claw on Rose's legs. At the most pathetic moment in the play the spectators were surprised to hear Geneviève de Brabant say to her son: 'Stop that, you little beast!'

A. Hugo, *Victor Hugo Raconté*, 1863.

JOHN RUSKIN
born February 1819.

The law was, that I should find my own amusement. No toys of any kind were at first allowed; − and the pity of my Croydon aunt for my monastic poverty in this respect was boundless. On one of my birthdays, thinking to overcome my mother's resolution by splendour of temptation, she bought the most radiant Punch and Judy, . . . all dressed in

scarlet and gold, and that would dance, tied to the leg of a chair. I must have been greatly impressed, for I remember well the look of the two figures, as my aunt herself exhibited their virtues. My mother was obliged to accept them; but afterwards quietly told me it was not right that I should have them; and I never saw them again.

Nor did I painfully wish, what I was never permitted for an instant to hope, or even imagine, the possession of such things as one saw in toy-shops. I had a bunch of keys to play with, as long as I was capable only of pleasure in what glittered and jingled; as I grew older, I had a cart, and a ball; and when I was five or six years old, two boxes of well-cut wooden bricks. With these modest, but, I still think, entirely sufficient possessions, and being always summarily whipped if I cried, did not do as I was bid, or tumbled on the stairs, I soon attained serene and secure methods of life and motion.

Ruskin, *Praeterita*, 1899.

ABRAHAM LINCOLN
born February 1809.

John Romine declared that as a boy 'Abe was awful lazy. He worked for me; was always reading and thinking; I used to get mad at him. He worked for me pulling fodder. I say

Abe was awful lazy. He would laugh and talk, and crack jokes, and tell stories all the time; didn't love work, but did dearly love his pay. He worked for me frequently, a few days only at a time. He said to me one day, that his father taught him to work, but never learned him to love it.'

Thayer, *Pioneer Boy*, 1882.

CATHERINE HUTTON
born February 1756.

The school, which till very recently had been the first in Birmingham, was kept by a Mrs and Miss Sawyer. The mother taught spelling and reading in the Bible, the daughter needlework, useful and ornamental, for sixpence a week. The governess was a kind-hearted old woman, who was obliged, or thought herself obliged, to scold sometimes. None of the scholars liked her; though I fully believe it was for no other reason than that she was old.

Miss Sawyer might be about thirty years of age; she was very handsome, very lady-like, and very good humoured. Mr Sawyer, her brother, was a dancing master . . .

After a while I became a pupil of Mr Sawyer, and no girl ever was or could be

fonder of dancing than myself; I used to jump about and cry. 'Oh, these are the joys of my dancing days.' Here, too, I learned to sing.

At ten years old I went to a writing school for one hour in a day, without quitting Mrs Sawyer's. My first attempt at writing was copying the printed letters of a battledore or horn-book. This was my first copybook and I remember being puzzled at the small letter *a*.

My school days were happy. Little was there to learn, and that little was easily learned.

Reminiscences of a Gentlewoman of the Last Century, edited by Mrs Catherine Hutton Beale, 1891, quoted by kind permission of Cornish Brothers Ltd.

GAMES
for the
FEBRUARY
BABY

RATHER than let children remain quiet when they come down in the morning on a rainy day, it is well to make them run round and round the breakfast-room table. They may at first do it unwillingly, but as the blood begins to circulate freely, they get into spirits, and laugh, and shout, and often break off into a merry game of Follow the Leader.

Kingston, *Infant Amusements*, 1867.

THE TOWN LOVERS

A game played by boys and girls. A girl is placed in the middle of a ring, and says the following lines, the names being altered to suit the party. She points to each one named, and

at the last line, the party selected immediately runs away, and if the girl catches him, he pays a forfeit, or the game is commenced again, the boy being placed in the middle ...

There is a girl of our town,
She often wears a flowered gown:
Tommy loves her night and day,

And Richard when he may,
And Johnny when he can:
I think Sam will be the man!
Popular Rhymes and Nursery Tales,
collected by Halliwell, 1849.

Touch each toe in turn, saying:
This pig went to market,
That pig staid at home,
This pig had roast meat,
That pig had none;
This pig went to the barn-door,
And cried Week, week, for more.
Mother Goose's Melody, London, 1817.

A
FEBRUARY
CHILD
IN
FICTION

CASTING my eyes along the street at a certain point of my progress, I beheld Trabb's boy approaching, lashing himself with an empty blue bag. Deeming that a serene and unconscious contemplation of him would best beseem me, and would be most likely to quell his evil mind, I advanced with that expression of countenance, and was rather congratulating myself on my success, when suddenly the

knees of Trabb's boy smote together, his hair uprose, his cap fell off, he trembled violently in every limb, staggered out into the road, and crying to the populace, 'Hold me! I'm so frightened!' feigned to be in a paroxysm of terror and contrition, occasioned by the dignity of my appearance. As I passed him, his teeth loudly chattered in his head, and with every mark of extreme humiliation, he prostrated himself in the dust.

This was a hard thing to bear, but this was nothing. I had not advanced another two hundred yards, when, to my inexpressible terror, amazement, and indignation, I again

beheld Trabb's boy approaching. He was coming round a narrow corner. His blue bag was slung over his shoulder, honest industry beamed in his eyes, a determination to proceed to Trabb's with cheerful briskness was indicated in his gait. With a shock he became aware of me, and was severely visited as before; but this time his motion was rotatory, and he staggered round and round me with knees more afflicted, and with uplifted hands as if beseeching for mercy. His sufferings were hailed with the greatest joy by a knot of spectators, and I felt utterly confounded.

Dickens, *Great Expectations*, 1860.

LETTERS
from
FEBRUARY
CHILDREN

PIERO DE' MEDICI, eldest son of Lorenzo the Magnificent, was born on 15th February, 1472. The first of these letters was dated 26th May, 1479, the others just 1479.

MAGNIFICENT FATHER,

Lucrezia and I are seeing who writes better. She writes to grandmother Lucrezia, and I, father, to you. The one that receives whatever he asks for is the winner. Up to now Lucrezia has got all she wanted. I who have written always in Latin to give my letters a more literary sound have not yet received the pony you promised me; so everybody laughs at me. Attend to it, then, Your Magnificence, so that she will not always be the winner.

MY MAGNIFICENT FATHER,

That pony has not come, and I am afraid that it will stay with you so long that Andrea will change it from an animal into a man, instead of fixing its hoof.

All of us are well and we are studying. Giovanni is starting spelling. You can see from this letter how my writing is. In Greek I keep in practice with Martino's help rather than advance. Giuliano just laughs and that is all; Lucrezia does sewing, singing and reading; Maddalena bumps her head against the wall but doesn't hurt herself; Luisa already says a few short words; Contessina makes noise wherever she is in the house. The others all do what they ought to do, and we need only your presence.

MY MAGNIFICENT FATHER,

I am afraid that something has happened to that pony, for if it were all right I am sure you would have sent me it as you said you would. So I ask you as a favour to tell me what has happened; for I think about it all day and at night, and until the pony gets here, I cannot have any peace. If that one cannot come, please send me a different one. For, as I have already told you in my letters, I am on foot here, and I sometimes have to go out with my friends. So attend to this, Your Magnificence.

MY MAGNIFICENT FATHER,

I am unable to tell you, Magnificent Father, how pleased I am to get the pony, and how much harder having him makes me work. He

is so beautiful and so perfect that the trumpet of Maron sounding at sundown on Olympus would scarcely do for singing his praises. You can imagine how much I love him; especially when he neighs for joy and makes the whole neighbourhood glad. I send you the thanks I owe you for such a wonderful gift, and I am going to try and repay you by being what you want me to be. Be sure of this. I promise to try as hard as I can. All of us are well, and we miss you. May God save you . . . 1479.

Your son PIERO at Gagliano.
Letterine d'un Bambino Fiorentino, Florence,
1887.

A LETTER FROM ANOTHER
FEBRUARY CHILD

Catherine Hutton was thirteen when she wrote this letter.

Kidderminster, March 4, 1769.

DEAR PAPPA AND MAMMA,

I am arrived safe at the end of my journey. I cried for the first mile, and then brightened up. Pray, Pappa, come and see me, I shall be very uneasy if you don't; but in some measure to make up for your absence, let me have the consolation of hearing from you almost every post. Mr Symonds has given me an ear of Indian maize, a sort of corn: it is very curious, in the shape of a cone. There are five hundred grains upon one ear when it is perfect, mine is not quite. We are engaged every day till next Saturday; on Wednesday at home in expectation of my Uncle and you; pray don't disappoint us. I hope you will then cast a short look towards Kidderminster, as last Wednesday you did a long one. Pappa, Mrs Hill has got a mighty pretty book. I should be glad if you would give me such a one; it is Dr Young's *Love of Fame*, a satirical piece. I believe he is a very good author; is not he? It cost 2s. unbound. I shall write to you so often that you will dread post day as I shall wish for it.

CATHERINE HUTTON.

Reminiscences of a Gentlewoman of the Last Century, edited by Mrs Catherine Hutton Beale, 1891, quoted by kind permission of Cornish Brothers Ltd.

RHYMES
for the
FEBRUARY
BABY

F EBRUARY brings the rain,
Thaws the frozen lake again.
              Sara Coleridge (1802–1852).

The rose is red, the violet's blue,
Carnation's sweet, and so are you.
Thou art my love, and I am thine;
I drew thee to my Valentine;
The lot was cast, and then I drew,
And fortune said it should be you.
                    Nursery Rhymes of England,
              collected by Halliwell, 1843.

Good morrow to you, Valentine!
Curl your locks as I do mine;
Two before and three behind;
Good morrow to you, Valentine:
> *Popular Rhymes and Nursery Tales,*
> collected by Halliwell, 1849.

Come to me, O ye children!
  And whisper in my ear
What the birds and the winds are singing
  In your sunny atmosphere.

For what are all our contrivings,
  And the wisdom of our books,

When compared with your caresses,
    And the gladness of your looks?

Ye are better than all the ballads
    That ever were sung or said;
For ye are living poems,
    And all the rest are dead.
                          Longfellow (1807–1882).

Hush thee, my babby,
Lie still with thy daddy,
Thy mammy has gone to the mill.
To grind thee some wheat,
To make thee some meat,
And so, my dear babby, lie still.
                    Nursery Rhymes of England,
                    collected by Halliwell, 1843.

A PRAYER

The prayer of St Thomas Aquinas, translated out of Latin into English by the most excellent princess Mary, daughter to the most high and mighty prince and princess king Henry 8th and queen Katharine his wife. In the year of our Lord God 1527, and the eleventh of her age.

'O merciful God! grant me to covet with an ardent mind those things which may please thee, to search them wisely, to know them truly, and to fulfil them perfectly to the laud and glory of thy name.'

From Strickland, *Lives of the Queens of England*, 1840.

GOODNIGHT
to the
FEBRUARY
BABY

WHEN the lights are out and you are dropping off to sleep do you make plans for your baby? If you could have chosen for yourself, what gifts would you have liked to have had? Are the gifts you would have liked for yourself those you would choose for your baby? Of course on the edge of sleep it is amusing to fancy that the tiny scrap in the bassinet will be a prime minister, a great ballerina, a millionaire, or a world-famous beauty, but when you wake and take your baby in your arms, will you want any of those fates for it? Almost certainly no, for what you will think as you look at the small face is, 'I don't want anything special for you, darling, I want you just the way you are.'

Noel Streatfeild